Advanced Mobile Cybersecurity and Digital Defense

How to Build a High-Level Mobile Security System Against Tracking, Surveillance, Malware, and Identity Theft

By Joe Correa

Published by Live Stronger Faster

Copyright © 2026 by Joe Correa

All rights reserved.

No part of this publication may be reproduced, distributed, or transmitted in any form or by any means—electronic, mechanical, photocopying, recording, or otherwise—without the prior written permission of the publisher, except in the case of brief quotations embodied in critical reviews and certain other noncommercial uses permitted by copyright law.

This book is for educational and informational purposes only. The author and publisher are not engaged in rendering legal, financial, or other professional advice. Readers should consult a qualified professional before making any financial decisions.

First Edition

Table of Contents

Introduction

Welcome to *Advanced Mobile Cybersecurity and Digital Defense: How to Build a High-Level Mobile Security System Against Tracking, Surveillance, Malware, and Identity Theft.*

Throughout this series, you have learned how to protect smartphones, secure applications, defend online accounts, use encryption tools, safeguard financial information, secure social media platforms, and protect family members from digital threats. Each book has focused on a specific area of mobile security, helping you develop practical skills that can be applied immediately in everyday life. This final volume brings everything together into a complete digital defense strategy designed for today's increasingly connected world.

Mobile devices have become the primary computing platform for billions of people. Smartphones now contain banking information, personal conversations, medical records, family photographs, business documents, passwords, location histories, and access to countless online accounts. For many people, their smartphone contains more sensitive information than their laptop, desktop computer, or even physical filing cabinet. As mobile technology has become more powerful, cybercriminals have increasingly shifted their attention toward mobile devices.

Modern cyber threats are far more sophisticated than they were only a few years ago. Attackers no longer rely solely on simple viruses or obvious scams. Today's threats include advanced spyware, surveillance software, identity theft operations, credential-stealing malware, fake mobile applications, phishing campaigns, social engineering attacks, location tracking systems, malicious Wi-Fi networks, and data harvesting platforms that collect enormous amounts of personal information. In many cases, victims are unaware that they have been compromised until significant damage has already occurred.

At the same time, digital surveillance has expanded dramatically. Governments, corporations, advertisers, data brokers, and cybercriminals all collect information about user behavior. Every app installed on a device, every website visited, every search performed, and every location traveled can potentially generate valuable data. Much of this information is collected automatically and often without users fully understanding how much of their digital lives are being monitored, analyzed, and stored.

The purpose of this book is not to create fear. Instead, it is to create awareness. Security begins with understanding. Once you understand how modern threats operate, you can make informed decisions that dramatically reduce your risk.

Cybersecurity is not about becoming paranoid. It is about becoming prepared.

One of the biggest misconceptions about cybersecurity is that only large organizations or wealthy individuals are targeted. In reality, cybercriminals often prefer ordinary users because they typically have fewer protections in place. Automated attack systems scan millions of devices every day looking for weaknesses. These attacks are not always directed at specific individuals. Instead, attackers search for vulnerable targets and exploit whatever opportunities they find.

Another misconception is that mobile security is purely a technical challenge. While technology certainly plays a major role, human behavior remains the most important factor. Many successful attacks occur because users click malicious links, install unsafe applications, reuse passwords, ignore security updates, connect to insecure networks, or share sensitive information without verifying who is requesting it. Technology can provide strong defenses, but informed decision-making remains the foundation of digital security.

As you progress through this book, you will learn how professional security experts approach mobile defense. Rather than relying on a single solution, they build multiple layers of protection. This concept is often called defense in depth. If one layer fails, additional layers continue providing protection. This approach greatly reduces the likelihood that a single mistake or vulnerability will lead to a major security incident.

You will learn how attackers collect information about potential victims and how to minimize your digital footprint. You will discover how mobile tracking systems work and how to limit unnecessary data collection. You will explore advanced authentication strategies that strengthen account security beyond traditional passwords. You will learn how to secure devices against malware, spyware, ransomware, and surveillance tools. You will also discover how to identify suspicious behavior that may indicate a compromise.

Identity theft remains one of the most damaging consequences of poor digital security. A compromised account can lead to financial losses, damaged credit, fraudulent transactions, privacy violations, and significant emotional stress. Fortunately, many identity theft incidents can be prevented through proactive security practices. Throughout this book, you will learn methods for protecting personal information before criminals have an opportunity to exploit it.

The rise of artificial intelligence has introduced both opportunities and challenges for cybersecurity. AI-powered systems can help detect threats, automate security monitoring, and improve defensive capabilities. At the same time, attackers are increasingly using artificial intelligence to create convincing phishing messages, automate scams, generate fake content, and identify vulnerabilities more efficiently. Understanding this evolving landscape is essential for anyone seeking long-term digital security.

Remote work, cloud computing, digital payments, online education, and social networking have permanently changed how people interact with technology. Mobile devices now serve as gateways to nearly every aspect of modern life. Because of this, cybersecurity can no longer be viewed as an optional skill. It has become a fundamental component of personal responsibility and digital citizenship.

One of the encouraging realities of cybersecurity is that significant improvements can often be achieved through relatively simple actions. Regular software updates, strong authentication practices, careful app selection, secure browsing habits, encrypted communications, and increased awareness of social engineering attacks can dramatically reduce risk. Security is rarely about perfection. Instead, it is about consistently making choices that improve resilience against threats.

Throughout this book, you will encounter practical strategies, real-world examples, and actionable recommendations. The goal is to provide knowledge that can be implemented immediately, regardless of your technical background. Whether you are a beginner seeking stronger personal protection or an advanced user interested in improving your digital defenses, the concepts presented here can help strengthen your overall security posture.

The cybersecurity landscape will continue evolving. New threats will emerge, technologies will change, and attackers will develop new techniques. However, the fundamental principles of security remain remarkably consistent. Awareness, preparation, layered defenses, risk management, and continuous learning form the foundation of effective protection. By mastering these principles, you can adapt to future challenges with confidence.

As the final book in the Mobile Security & App Protection Academy series, this volume serves as a comprehensive guide for building a complete mobile defense system. It combines lessons from previous books while introducing advanced strategies for protecting privacy, securing communications, preventing surveillance, defending against sophisticated attacks, and maintaining control over your digital identity.

Your smartphone is more than a device. It is an extension of your personal, professional, and financial life. Protecting it means protecting your future opportunities, your privacy, your relationships, and your peace of mind. The knowledge contained in this book is designed to help you take control of your digital environment and build security habits that will serve you for years to come.

The journey toward stronger cybersecurity begins with awareness, grows through education, and succeeds through consistent action. Let us begin building your advanced mobile cybersecurity and digital defense system.

Chapter 1

Building Your Personal Mobile Security Architecture

Most people think of cybersecurity as a collection of individual tools. They install an antivirus application, create a password, enable a few security settings, and assume they are protected. Unfortunately, modern cybersecurity no longer works this way. Cybercriminals have become highly organized, automated, and sophisticated. They understand that every security system contains weaknesses, and they look for the easiest path to exploitation. Because of this, effective protection requires a complete security architecture rather than a collection of disconnected tools.

A security architecture is a structured system of protective layers that work together. Just as a modern building includes locks, alarms, cameras, reinforced doors, fire suppression systems, and emergency exits, a secure mobile device requires multiple defensive components. Each layer serves a different purpose. If one layer fails, the remaining layers continue protecting the device and its owner.

The first layer of mobile security is physical security. Before discussing hackers, malware, or surveillance, it is important to understand that physical access remains one of the fastest ways to compromise a device. If someone gains possession of an unlocked phone, they may access messages, banking apps, passwords, email accounts, photographs, and private documents within minutes. This is why every device should be protected with a strong passcode, biometric authentication, and automatic screen locking.

Strong authentication serves as the second layer of protection. Many people continue using simple passwords that can be guessed through personal information, dictionary attacks, or credential databases obtained from previous data breaches. Strong authentication combines unique passwords with multi-factor authentication. This creates an additional barrier that significantly increases security. Even if a password becomes compromised, attackers still need access to the secondary verification method.

The third layer focuses on software integrity. Every application installed on a smartphone introduces potential risk. Some applications contain vulnerabilities. Others collect excessive information. In rare cases, applications may contain malicious code intentionally designed to steal information or monitor user activity. For this reason, users should regularly evaluate installed applications, remove unnecessary software, and download apps only from trusted sources.

Software updates form another critical component of security architecture. Attackers frequently target known vulnerabilities that manufacturers have already fixed. Unfortunately, many users delay updates for weeks or months, leaving devices exposed to threats that could have been prevented. Every update represents an opportunity to close security gaps before criminals exploit them.

Network security provides another important defensive layer. Smartphones constantly connect to cellular networks, home Wi-Fi networks, workplace networks, public hotspots, Bluetooth devices, and internet services. Every connection creates potential exposure. Users should carefully evaluate the networks they join and avoid transmitting sensitive information through unknown or unsecured connections whenever possible.

Privacy protection serves as a defensive layer against tracking and surveillance. Many applications request access to location information, contacts, microphones, cameras, calendars, and other sensitive data. While some requests are legitimate, others exceed what is necessary for the application's functionality. Reviewing permissions regularly helps reduce unnecessary data collection and minimizes privacy risks.

Data protection is equally important. Even the most secure device can experience theft, loss, hardware failure, or accidental damage. Maintaining encrypted backups ensures that valuable information remains accessible while preventing unauthorized access. A strong backup strategy protects against both security incidents and unexpected technical failures.

One of the most overlooked aspects of security architecture is user awareness. Technology can provide powerful defenses, but human decisions often determine whether attacks succeed or fail. Cybercriminals frequently use social engineering rather than technical exploits because manipulating people is often easier than defeating security systems. Learning to recognize suspicious messages, fraudulent websites, fake support requests, and phishing attempts significantly strengthens overall protection.

Threat modeling represents an advanced cybersecurity concept that can greatly improve decision-making. Threat modeling involves identifying the specific risks most relevant to an individual. A business executive, journalist, healthcare professional, student, and retiree may face different threats. Understanding personal risk allows users to prioritize defensive measures more effectively.

For example, someone who frequently conducts financial transactions may focus heavily on banking security and identity theft prevention. A parent may prioritize child protection tools and family monitoring systems. A business owner may focus on secure communications and protecting customer information. Security becomes far more effective when it aligns with actual risks.

Another important principle involves minimizing the attack surface. Every application, account, service, and connected device creates an additional opportunity for compromise. Reducing unnecessary complexity often improves security. Unused applications should be removed. Dormant accounts should be closed. Permissions should be limited to only what is necessary. Simplicity often enhances protection.

Modern cybersecurity also requires continuous improvement. Threats evolve constantly. Security strategies that worked several years ago may no longer provide adequate protection today. Users should regularly review their security settings, evaluate emerging threats, and update their defenses accordingly. Security is a process rather than a destination.

The ultimate goal of mobile security architecture is resilience. Perfect security does not exist. Every device contains potential vulnerabilities. Every system faces some degree of risk.

However, by building multiple protective layers and continuously improving defenses, users can dramatically reduce the likelihood of becoming victims of cybercrime, surveillance, malware, or identity theft.

Michael received a notification from his bank regarding unusual activity

Michael considered himself reasonably careful with technology. He used a password on his smartphone, downloaded apps from official stores, and occasionally installed updates. Like millions of other users, he believed these simple actions were enough to keep him safe. He had never experienced a major cybersecurity incident and assumed serious attacks only happened to corporations or high-profile individuals.

One Monday morning, Michael received a notification from his bank regarding unusual activity. Several online purchases had been attempted using his account information. Although the transactions were ultimately blocked, the alert immediately raised concerns. He changed his banking password and assumed the problem had been resolved.

A few days later, he noticed unfamiliar login attempts on one of his email accounts. Shortly afterward, a social media platform requested that he verify his identity because suspicious access had been detected. The incidents seemed unrelated, but together they created a troubling pattern.

Concerned, Michael contacted a cybersecurity consultant named Sarah. After reviewing his situation, Sarah explained that cybersecurity incidents rarely occur in isolation. Criminals often gather small pieces of information from multiple sources before attempting larger attacks. What appeared to be separate events could actually be connected.

Sarah began evaluating Michael's digital habits. She discovered that he reused similar passwords across multiple accounts. Several applications had access to location services even though they did not require it. Many installed apps had not been used in years. His smartphone operating system was several months behind on updates. Public Wi-Fi networks had been used regularly while traveling.

None of these issues alone guaranteed compromise. However, together they created numerous opportunities for attackers. Sarah compared the situation to a house with several unlocked windows. An intruder only needed one successful entry point.

Rather than focusing on a single solution, Sarah introduced Michael to the concept of security architecture. She explained that strong cybersecurity depends on layers of protection working together. The goal was not simply to stop one specific threat but to create a resilient system capable of resisting multiple forms of attack.

They began by strengthening authentication. Every important account received a unique password generated through a password manager. Multi-factor authentication was enabled wherever possible. Recovery methods were reviewed and updated.

Next, they examined installed applications. Dozens of unnecessary apps were removed. Permissions were reviewed carefully. Location tracking was disabled for many programs that had no legitimate need to know Michael's whereabouts. Several suspicious applications were uninstalled entirely.

Software updates were then applied across all devices. Sarah explained how many attacks exploit vulnerabilities that manufacturers have already fixed. Keeping systems current represented one of the simplest and most effective security measures available.

Network security became the next priority. Michael learned how public Wi-Fi networks could expose users to unnecessary risk. He began using trusted networks whenever possible and became more cautious about transmitting sensitive information while connected to unfamiliar systems.

As the weeks passed, Michael noticed something unexpected. He no longer felt anxious about cybersecurity. Instead of reacting to threats after they appeared, he had developed a proactive strategy. His defenses were organized, monitored, and continuously improved.

Several months later, Michael received another phishing message disguised as a banking notification. In the past, he might have clicked the link without much thought. This time, he immediately recognized warning signs. The sender address appeared unusual. The message created a false sense of urgency. The link destination did not match the official website.

Rather than becoming a victim, Michael reported the message and deleted it. The attack failed because his awareness had improved.

Over time, his confidence grew. He understood that cybersecurity was not about fear. It was about preparation. Every protective layer reduced risk. Every informed decision strengthened resilience. Every security habit contributed to long-term protection.

Looking back, Michael realized the most valuable lesson Sarah had taught him was that cybersecurity is not a product. It is a system. Passwords, updates, privacy settings, backups, authentication tools, and awareness all work together to create meaningful protection.

His smartphone still connected him to friends, family, work, banking, entertainment, and countless online services. The difference was that he now controlled those connections instead of leaving them vulnerable to chance. Through a carefully constructed security architecture, he had transformed a collection of disconnected defenses into a complete digital protection system capable of adapting to the evolving threats of the modern world.

Chapter 2

Defending Against Mobile Tracking, Surveillance, and Data Collection

One of the greatest cybersecurity challenges facing mobile device users today is not malware, hacking, or even identity theft. It is the massive amount of tracking and surveillance that occurs every day, often without the user's full awareness. Modern smartphones are powerful devices that constantly communicate with applications, websites, wireless networks, cloud services, advertising platforms, and data analytics companies. Every interaction can generate information about who you are, where you go, what you do, who you communicate with, and what interests you. Understanding how mobile tracking works is essential for building an advanced mobile security system.

Many people assume that tracking only occurs when a GPS application is actively being used. In reality, location information can be collected from numerous sources. GPS signals, Wi-Fi networks, Bluetooth beacons, cell towers, application permissions, advertising identifiers, photos containing metadata, and even nearby devices can reveal information about a user's location. Individually, these data points may seem insignificant. However, when combined over time, they can create an extremely detailed picture of a person's daily routines and behaviors.

Location tracking has legitimate uses. Navigation applications help users reach destinations. Weather applications provide local forecasts. Delivery services rely on location data to complete orders. Emergency services use location information to assist people in need. Problems arise when data collection exceeds what is reasonably necessary or when information is shared with third parties without clear user understanding.

Many applications collect far more information than users realize. Some apps monitor usage habits, device characteristics, search activity, purchasing behavior, and interaction patterns. This information may be used to personalize advertising, improve products, conduct market research, or generate revenue through data partnerships. While some forms of data collection are disclosed in privacy policies, many users never review these documents or understand the extent of the information being collected.

Advertising identifiers play a significant role in mobile tracking ecosystems. Both Android and iPhone devices provide unique identifiers that allow advertisers to recognize devices across applications and websites. These identifiers help companies build profiles based on browsing habits, interests, and behavior patterns. While advertising identifiers do not always contain personal names, they can still reveal substantial information about an individual's activities.

Reducing advertising-based tracking begins with understanding available privacy controls. Modern operating systems provide settings that allow users to limit ad personalization, reset advertising identifiers, and restrict cross-application tracking. While these settings do not eliminate all forms of tracking, they significantly reduce the amount of information available to advertising networks.

Application permissions represent another major area of concern. Every permission granted to an application creates an opportunity for information collection. Some permissions are necessary for functionality. A navigation app requires location access. A camera app requires camera access. However, users should carefully evaluate requests that seem unrelated to the app's purpose. A flashlight app requesting access to contacts or a simple game requesting microphone access should prompt closer examination.

The principle of least privilege is an important cybersecurity concept that applies directly to mobile devices. This principle states that applications should receive only the minimum permissions required to perform their intended functions.

Limiting permissions reduces the amount of information available for collection and decreases potential exposure if an application becomes compromised.

Metadata is another often-overlooked source of information leakage. Metadata is information about data rather than the data itself. For example, photographs may contain information about when and where they were taken. Documents may include author information, modification history, and device details. Messages may reveal timestamps, locations, and communication patterns. Even when the content itself remains private, metadata can provide valuable intelligence to observers.

Social media applications are particularly effective at collecting behavioral information. Every like, comment, share, search, follow, and interaction contributes to a digital profile. Over time, these profiles become increasingly detailed and accurate. Social platforms can often predict interests, preferences, habits, and behaviors based on activity patterns. Understanding this reality allows users to make more informed decisions about what they share and how they engage online.

Wireless technologies also contribute to tracking risks. Bluetooth devices continuously communicate with nearby equipment. Public Wi-Fi networks may collect connection information. Smart devices within homes and workplaces generate additional data streams. Users should disable wireless services when not needed and regularly review connected devices to ensure they recognize all active connections.

Data brokers represent another significant component of the modern information economy. These organizations collect information from various sources, combine datasets, and create detailed consumer profiles. Information may include addresses, purchasing behavior, demographic details, online activity, and public records. While regulations vary by jurisdiction, users should understand that substantial information about them may already exist within commercial databases.

Surveillance concerns extend beyond commercial tracking. Cybercriminals, stalkers, abusive partners, and malicious actors may attempt to install spyware or monitoring software on mobile devices. These tools can collect messages, call logs, locations, photographs, browsing history, and other sensitive information. While advanced spyware is relatively rare, users should remain alert for unusual device behavior such as rapid battery drain, unexplained overheating, excessive data usage, or unknown applications.

Protecting against surveillance requires a layered approach. Strong device authentication prevents unauthorized access. Operating system updates reduce vulnerability exposure. Application reviews help identify suspicious software. Permission audits limit unnecessary information sharing. Encrypted communications protect sensitive conversations. Together, these measures create meaningful barriers against both commercial and malicious surveillance.

Privacy and security are closely related but distinct concepts. Security focuses on preventing unauthorized access. Privacy focuses on controlling how information is collected, used, and shared. A secure device may still generate extensive data collection if privacy controls are not properly configured. Advanced mobile cybersecurity requires attention to both objectives.

Developing privacy awareness is one of the most valuable skills users can cultivate. Before installing applications, granting permissions, sharing information, or enabling features, users should ask whether the benefit justifies the information being provided. Small decisions made consistently over time can significantly reduce unnecessary exposure.

The goal of privacy protection is not complete invisibility. Modern life requires digital participation. Instead, the objective is informed control. By understanding how tracking systems operate and implementing practical safeguards, users can enjoy the benefits of technology while maintaining greater authority over their personal information and digital identities.

She wondered how advertisers knew about her interests so quickly

Emma considered herself an ordinary smartphone user. She used social media, online shopping apps, navigation services, messaging platforms, and streaming services. Like most people, she appreciated convenience and rarely thought about the information being collected behind the scenes.

One afternoon, Emma mentioned to a friend that she was considering taking a vacation to the mountains. The conversation took place in person while they were having lunch. She did not search for travel destinations online, visit tourism websites, or browse airline tickets. Yet later that evening, she noticed advertisements for mountain resorts, hiking equipment, and cabin rentals appearing across multiple applications.

The experience felt strange. She wondered how advertisers knew about her interests so quickly. Curious, she began researching digital privacy and discovered how complex modern tracking systems had become.

Her research introduced her to David, a cybersecurity consultant who specialized in privacy protection. During their first meeting, David explained that tracking does not always require listening to conversations. Instead, companies often make highly accurate predictions using data collected from searches, locations, purchases, social interactions, browsing habits, and behavioral patterns.

David helped Emma review her smartphone settings. What they discovered surprised her. More than fifty applications had location access. Several apps could access her contacts. Numerous programs had permission to use the microphone, camera, and photo library. Many of these permissions had been granted years earlier and never reviewed.

Together, they began auditing her device. Applications that no longer served a useful purpose were removed. Permissions were restricted to only what was necessary. Background location tracking was disabled for most apps. Advertising settings were adjusted to reduce personalized tracking.

The process opened Emma's eyes to how much information she had been sharing unknowingly. Every app seemed to request access to something. Every service collected some form of data. She realized that convenience often came with hidden costs.

A few weeks later, Emma received a message from a friend who believed her social media account had been compromised. Several unusual posts had appeared, and login notifications showed access from unfamiliar locations. Fortunately, Emma had enabled multi-factor authentication during her security review. Attackers possessed her password from an older data breach but could not access the account without the secondary verification step.

The incident reinforced the value of proactive security measures. Rather than waiting until something went wrong, Emma had already strengthened her defenses.

As her awareness grew, she began making different choices. Before installing applications, she reviewed permissions carefully. She disabled unnecessary wireless services when traveling. She used encrypted messaging platforms for sensitive conversations. She became more selective about what she shared online.

Months later, Emma attended a technology conference where cybersecurity experts discussed privacy, surveillance, and digital rights. Listening to the presentations, she realized that privacy was not simply about hiding information. It was about maintaining control over personal decisions and preventing others from building detailed profiles without consent.

One speaker compared personal information to currency. Every piece of data had value. Companies competed to collect it. Criminals attempted to steal it. Advertisers sought to analyze it. The challenge for users was deciding when that information should be exchanged and when it should remain private.

Inspired by what she learned, Emma helped friends and family review their own devices. Many were surprised by the number of permissions granted to applications. Some discovered unused accounts they had forgotten existed. Others found outdated software that needed immediate updates.

Over time, Emma became known among her friends as the person to ask about privacy settings and mobile security. She never considered herself a technical expert, but she understood something important: cybersecurity begins with awareness.

The most significant change was psychological. Emma no longer viewed technology as something that simply happened to her. She understood the systems operating behind the scenes. She recognized the value of her information. Most importantly, she realized she had choices.

Her smartphone continued to provide convenience, entertainment, communication, and productivity. The difference was that she now used those tools on her own terms. Through education, awareness, and consistent action, she transformed herself from a passive participant in the digital ecosystem into an informed and empowered user.

The lesson she shared most often was simple. Privacy is not about disappearing from the digital world. It is about understanding how information flows and deciding what should remain under your control. In a world increasingly driven by data, that knowledge had become one of the most valuable forms of security available.

Chapter 3

Advanced Authentication and Identity Theft Prevention

One of the most valuable assets a person possesses in the digital age is not money, property, or even technology itself. It is identity. Nearly every aspect of modern life relies on digital identity systems. Banking accounts, email platforms, social media profiles, healthcare portals, government services, online shopping accounts, cloud storage systems, investment platforms, and mobile payment applications all depend on verifying who a user is. Because of this, cybercriminals devote enormous effort toward stealing, impersonating, and exploiting digital identities.

Identity theft has evolved significantly over the past two decades. Early forms of identity theft often involved stolen mail, physical documents, or direct financial fraud. Today, identity theft is primarily a digital crime. Attackers collect information through data breaches, phishing campaigns, malware infections, social engineering attacks, account compromises, and information purchased on underground criminal marketplaces. Once sufficient information is obtained, criminals may open financial accounts, apply for loans, access existing services, conduct fraudulent transactions, or impersonate victims for various forms of exploitation.

The foundation of identity protection begins with authentication. Authentication is the process of proving that a person is who they claim to be. Every time a user logs into an account, authentication occurs. Unfortunately, many authentication systems remain vulnerable because users continue relying on weak passwords, reused credentials, and outdated security practices.

Passwords remain the most common authentication method despite their limitations. Many users select passwords based on names, birthdays, pets, favorite sports teams, or other easily guessed information. Attackers understand these tendencies and use automated tools capable of testing millions of password combinations within minutes. Passwords that appear secure to humans may be surprisingly vulnerable to modern cracking techniques.

Strong passwords should be unique, lengthy, and difficult to predict. Security experts increasingly recommend passphrases rather than traditional passwords. A passphrase combines multiple unrelated words into a longer sequence that is easier to remember while remaining resistant to automated attacks. Length often contributes more to security than complexity alone. A long passphrase can provide stronger protection than a short password filled with special characters.

Password reuse creates another major vulnerability. When users reuse passwords across multiple accounts, a compromise affecting one service can expose many others. Criminals routinely purchase stolen credential databases and test those credentials against numerous websites. This technique, known as credential stuffing, remains highly successful because password reuse continues to be common.

Password managers provide an effective solution to this challenge. These tools generate unique credentials for every account and store them securely within encrypted vaults. Instead of memorizing dozens or hundreds of passwords, users only need to protect a single master credential. Password managers significantly reduce password reuse while improving overall account security.

Multi-factor authentication represents one of the most important advancements in account protection. Traditional authentication relies on something a user knows, such as a password. Multi-factor authentication adds additional verification factors. These may include something a user possesses, such as a smartphone, or something a user is, such as a fingerprint or facial scan.

Even if attackers obtain a password, multi-factor authentication can prevent unauthorized access. The criminal must also possess the secondary authentication factor. This additional barrier dramatically reduces successful account compromises and is among the most effective defenses available to ordinary users.

Authentication applications generally provide stronger protection than text-message verification. While SMS-based authentication is better than passwords alone, attackers have developed methods for intercepting messages, conducting SIM-swapping attacks, or redirecting verification codes. Authentication applications generate temporary codes directly on trusted devices and reduce reliance on vulnerable communication channels.

Biometric authentication has become increasingly common on mobile devices. Fingerprint scanners, facial recognition systems, and other biometric technologies offer convenience while improving security. However, users should understand both their strengths and limitations. Biometric systems are generally effective but should be viewed as one layer within a broader security strategy rather than a complete solution.

Account recovery procedures deserve careful attention. Many users focus heavily on passwords while overlooking recovery options. Attackers frequently target recovery mechanisms because they often provide alternative paths into accounts. Security questions based on publicly available information may be vulnerable. Recovery email addresses should be secured with the same diligence as primary accounts.

Email security is particularly important because email often serves as the central hub for account recovery. If criminals gain access to a user's email account, they may reset passwords for numerous connected services. Protecting email accounts should therefore be considered a top priority within any identity protection strategy.

Phishing remains one of the most effective identity theft techniques. Rather than attacking technical systems directly, phishing attacks target human psychology. Criminals create messages designed to appear legitimate while encouraging users to reveal credentials, financial information, or verification codes. Modern phishing campaigns often imitate banks, delivery companies, government agencies, employers, and popular online services.

Recognizing phishing attempts requires attention to detail. Users should verify sender addresses, inspect links carefully, question urgent requests, and avoid providing sensitive information through unsolicited communications. Healthy skepticism serves as a valuable defense against social engineering attacks.

Data breaches represent another significant source of identity theft risk. Even organizations with substantial security resources occasionally experience breaches that expose customer information. Users cannot fully prevent such incidents, but they can reduce their impact through unique passwords, multi-factor authentication, and regular account monitoring.

Credit monitoring provides an additional layer of protection. Many identity theft incidents involve unauthorized financial activity. Monitoring credit reports helps users detect suspicious accounts, inquiries, or transactions before significant damage occurs. Early detection often reduces both financial losses and recovery efforts.

Identity theft prevention also includes limiting unnecessary information exposure. Criminals often gather information from social media profiles, public databases, online forums, and other publicly accessible sources. Sharing less information reduces opportunities for attackers to build detailed victim profiles.

Digital identity protection requires ongoing vigilance rather than one-time actions. Threats evolve continuously. New attack methods emerge regularly. Effective security depends upon maintaining strong habits, reviewing accounts periodically, and adapting to changing risks.

Ultimately, authentication and identity protection are about maintaining control. Every security measure contributes to a broader objective: ensuring that only authorized individuals can access sensitive information and digital resources. By implementing layered authentication strategies and understanding how identity theft occurs, users can dramatically strengthen their defenses against one of the most persistent threats in the digital world.

Daniel received a call from his credit card company

Daniel had always considered identity theft something that happened to other people. He paid his bills on time, used online banking, maintained a respectable credit score, and generally avoided suspicious websites. As far as he was concerned, cybersecurity was important but not something that required constant attention.

One Friday afternoon, Daniel received a call from his credit card company. A representative informed him that several unusual transactions had been detected in another state. Fortunately, the fraud department had identified the activity quickly and blocked additional purchases. Daniel assumed his credit card information had simply been stolen and expected the situation to be resolved easily.

The following week brought additional surprises. A bank notified him of an attempted loan application. An online retailer reported suspicious login attempts. His email provider sent alerts indicating access attempts from unfamiliar devices. What initially appeared to be a single incident was rapidly becoming something much larger.

Concerned about the growing pattern, Daniel contacted a cybersecurity consultant named Rebecca. During their first meeting, Rebecca explained that identity theft often develops gradually. Criminals gather information from multiple sources over time, eventually accumulating enough data to impersonate victims effectively.

Rebecca began reviewing Daniel's digital security practices. The results revealed several weaknesses. Like many users, Daniel reused variations of the same password across numerous accounts. His email account lacked multi-factor authentication. Several online accounts contained outdated recovery information. Many services still relied on security questions based on easily discoverable personal details.

Rebecca explained how criminals frequently purchase stolen credentials from previous data breaches. Automated tools then test those credentials across countless websites. If users reuse passwords, attackers may gain access to multiple accounts with minimal effort.

Together, they began strengthening Daniel's defenses. A password manager was installed. Every major account received a unique credential. Multi-factor authentication was enabled across financial institutions, email services, cloud storage platforms, and social media accounts. Recovery settings were reviewed carefully.

As they worked, Rebecca emphasized an important lesson. Security was not about creating an impenetrable fortress. It was about increasing the difficulty of attack. Criminals often seek easy targets. Every additional layer of protection increases the likelihood that attackers will move on to less protected victims.

Several weeks later, Daniel received a convincing email that appeared to originate from his bank. The message warned of suspicious activity and instructed him to verify account information immediately. Before his recent security training, he likely would have clicked the link without hesitation.

This time, he paused.

Examining the message closely, he noticed subtle inconsistencies. The sender address contained unusual characters. The link destination did not match the bank's official domain. The language attempted to create urgency and panic. Instead of responding, Daniel contacted the bank directly through official channels. The email was fraudulent.

The experience demonstrated how awareness complements technology. Security tools provide protection, but informed judgment remains equally important.

Months later, Daniel enrolled in a credit monitoring service and began reviewing financial reports regularly. During one routine review, he discovered an unauthorized inquiry connected to a lender he had never contacted. Because the issue was identified early, corrective action occurred before significant damage could develop.

The incident reinforced another lesson. Detection is as important as prevention. Even strong security measures cannot eliminate all risk. Regular monitoring allows users to identify problems before they escalate.

As time passed, Daniel became increasingly confident in his ability to manage digital risks. He no longer viewed cybersecurity as a confusing technical field reserved for experts. Instead, he understood it as a collection of practical habits and informed decisions.

Friends occasionally asked why he spent time managing passwords, reviewing account settings, and monitoring security alerts. His answer was simple. The inconvenience of prevention was far smaller than the consequences of recovery.

One evening, a coworker experienced a major identity theft incident involving fraudulent credit accounts and compromised online services. Watching the lengthy recovery process reminded Daniel how fortunate he had been to address his vulnerabilities early.

Reflecting on his experience, Daniel realized that identity protection was not merely about safeguarding money. It protected reputation, opportunities, privacy, and peace of mind. Every account represented part of his digital identity. Every security measure helped preserve control over that identity.

The most valuable lesson Rebecca taught him was that identity theft prevention begins long before criminals attempt an attack. It begins with strong authentication, careful information management, and consistent security habits. By taking responsibility for his digital identity, Daniel had transformed himself from a vulnerable target into a resilient and informed defender of his personal information.

In a world where digital identities increasingly shape financial, professional, and personal opportunities, that transformation proved to be one of the most important investments he could make in his future.

Chapter 4

Detecting, Preventing, and Responding to Mobile Malware and Spyware

Mobile devices have become the center of modern life. They store personal photographs, private conversations, financial information, work documents, passwords, health records, and access to countless online accounts. Because smartphones contain so much valuable information, they have become attractive targets for cybercriminals. One of the most significant threats facing mobile users today is malware and spyware. Understanding how these threats operate and how to defend against them is a critical component of advanced mobile cybersecurity.

Malware is a broad term used to describe malicious software designed to damage systems, steal information, disrupt operations, or provide unauthorized access to attackers. Spyware is a specialized category of malware that focuses on monitoring user activity and collecting information without consent. While many users associate malware with traditional desktop computers, mobile devices have become increasingly common targets because of their widespread use and the valuable information they contain.

Cybercriminals distribute mobile malware through various methods. Malicious applications, phishing messages, infected websites, compromised advertisements, fraudulent software updates, social engineering attacks, and unsafe downloads are among the most common infection vectors. Attackers often disguise malicious content as legitimate software or trusted communications to encourage users to lower their defenses.

One of the most effective malware delivery methods involves fake applications. Attackers create programs that appear useful, entertaining, or beneficial while secretly containing malicious code. These applications may imitate popular games, productivity tools, financial services, or social media platforms. Once installed, they may collect information, display fraudulent advertisements, steal credentials, or provide remote access to attackers.

Users should carefully evaluate applications before installation. Reviewing developer information, reading user feedback, checking download counts, and examining requested permissions can help identify suspicious software. While official app stores generally provide better security than unofficial sources, malicious applications occasionally bypass screening processes. Users should therefore maintain healthy skepticism even when downloading from trusted platforms.

Permissions provide valuable clues regarding application behavior. Every app requests access to specific device functions. Some permissions are necessary for intended functionality, while others may indicate excessive data collection. For example, a photo editing app may reasonably require access to stored images, but it may not need access to contacts, call logs, or location data. Reviewing permissions before installation and periodically afterward helps reduce unnecessary exposure.

Spyware represents one of the most concerning mobile threats because it often operates silently. Unlike ransomware or disruptive malware, spyware typically attempts to avoid detection. Its goal is information collection rather than immediate damage. Spyware may record messages, monitor browsing activity, capture screenshots, track locations, log keystrokes, access microphones, or monitor communications.

In some cases, spyware is installed by cybercriminals seeking financial gain. In other situations, spyware may be used by stalkers, abusive partners, corporate spies, or other individuals attempting to monitor victims without their knowledge. Understanding these risks is essential for recognizing potential warning signs.

Several symptoms may indicate malware or spyware infections. Unusual battery drain often occurs because malicious software continuously runs in the background. Excessive data usage may result from stolen information being transmitted to external servers. Unexpected device overheating, unexplained performance degradation, unusual pop-up advertisements, unauthorized account activity, and unfamiliar installed applications may also indicate compromise.

While these symptoms do not automatically confirm infection, they warrant investigation. Many legitimate issues can produce similar behavior. However, users should never ignore persistent abnormalities. Early detection often limits damage and simplifies recovery.

Software updates play a vital role in malware prevention. Operating system developers regularly identify and patch vulnerabilities that attackers might otherwise exploit. Delaying updates leaves devices exposed to known weaknesses. Automatic updates provide one of the simplest and most effective security measures available to mobile users.

Secure browsing habits also contribute significantly to malware prevention. Many attacks begin when users click suspicious links, visit compromised websites, or download files from untrusted sources. Users should verify website authenticity, avoid unsolicited downloads, and exercise caution when responding to unexpected messages or offers.

Phishing attacks frequently serve as malware delivery mechanisms. Attackers send messages that appear to originate from trusted organizations, encouraging users to click links or install software. These messages often create urgency by claiming accounts are locked, payments are overdue, or security incidents require immediate action. Recognizing these tactics helps users avoid becoming victims.

Mobile security applications can provide additional protection by identifying known threats and monitoring device activity. While no security solution is perfect, reputable security software can enhance visibility and provide early warnings regarding suspicious behavior. Users should select security products from established providers and keep them updated regularly.

Backing up important information is another essential defensive strategy. Even if malware compromises a device, secure backups help preserve valuable data and simplify recovery. Backups should be performed regularly and stored securely using trusted cloud services or encrypted local storage.

If malware infection is suspected, users should act quickly. Disconnecting from networks may help limit data transmission. Reviewing recently installed applications can identify potential sources of compromise. Running security scans, updating software, changing passwords, and monitoring account activity are important response measures. In severe cases, performing a factory reset may be necessary to restore device integrity.

Incident response is often overlooked by ordinary users. Many people focus exclusively on prevention while assuming attacks will never occur. In reality, even well-protected systems may experience security incidents. Preparing response procedures in advance improves recovery outcomes and reduces panic during stressful situations.

Advanced cybersecurity requires a proactive mindset. Rather than waiting for obvious problems to appear, users should continuously monitor device health, review account activity, evaluate installed applications, and remain informed about emerging threats. Small security habits performed consistently provide substantial protection over time.

The goal of malware defense is not achieving perfect security. No system can guarantee complete protection against every threat. Instead, the objective is risk reduction. By combining awareness, technology, safe habits, software updates, backups, and incident response planning, users can significantly reduce their vulnerability to malware and spyware attacks.

Understanding these principles transforms cybersecurity from a reactive process into a proactive defense strategy. Knowledge empowers users to identify threats early, respond effectively, and maintain greater control over their digital lives in an increasingly complex threat environment.

Ryan installed the application

Ryan considered himself technologically savvy. He worked remotely, managed investments through mobile applications, communicated with clients through his smartphone, and stored important personal and professional information on his device. Because he used technology daily, he assumed he could recognize most cyber threats.

One evening, while browsing online, Ryan encountered an advertisement promoting a free productivity application. The app promised advanced note-taking features, AI-powered organization tools, and seamless synchronization across devices. The description appeared professional, and the screenshots looked convincing.

Without much hesitation, Ryan installed the application.

Initially, everything seemed normal. The software functioned as advertised, and Ryan quickly integrated it into his daily routine. Over the following weeks, however, subtle changes began appearing. His smartphone battery drained faster than usual. Data usage increased unexpectedly. The device occasionally became warm even when idle.

Ryan attributed these issues to normal wear and tear. Smartphones, after all, sometimes slow down with age.

Several weeks later, he received notifications from multiple online services indicating login attempts from unfamiliar locations. One account reported a successful login from another country. Another platform requested password verification due to suspicious activity.

Concerned, Ryan began investigating.

He reviewed recent account activity and discovered several unauthorized access attempts. While no major damage had occurred, the pattern suggested someone possessed at least some of his credentials. Unsure how this happened, Ryan contacted a cybersecurity specialist named Olivia.

Olivia started by reviewing Ryan's device and security practices. She asked about recent software installations, unusual behavior, and account activity. When Ryan mentioned the productivity app, Olivia became interested.

After conducting a detailed analysis, she discovered that the application contained spyware functionality hidden beneath its legitimate features. While the app performed basic productivity tasks, it also collected device information, monitored certain activities, and transmitted data to external servers.

Ryan was shocked.

The application looked professional. It functioned correctly. It had positive reviews. Yet beneath the surface, it was quietly gathering information.

Olivia explained that modern malware often prioritizes stealth over disruption. The goal is not necessarily to damage the device immediately. Instead, attackers seek long-term access to valuable information. By remaining undetected, spyware can operate for extended periods.

Together, they began responding to the incident. The application was removed. Security scans were performed. Passwords were changed across important accounts. Multi-factor authentication was enabled wherever possible.

Device permissions were reviewed carefully. Monitoring systems were established to detect future anomalies.

The experience served as a powerful lesson.

Ryan realized that cybersecurity threats rarely resemble movie-style hacking scenes. There are often no flashing warnings, dramatic alerts, or obvious signs of compromise. Instead, attacks frequently occur quietly and gradually. Small clues accumulate over time until a larger pattern becomes visible.

Over the following months, Ryan adopted stronger security habits. He researched applications before installation. He reviewed permissions carefully. He enabled automatic updates. He monitored account activity regularly. Most importantly, he developed a healthy sense of skepticism.

One afternoon, he received a text message claiming to be from a package delivery service. The message stated that a shipment could not be delivered and instructed him to install a tracking application. The link appeared legitimate at first glance.

Before clicking, Ryan paused.

His previous experience reminded him that attackers often exploit trust and urgency. Rather than following the link, he visited the shipping company's official website directly. There was no delivery issue. The message was fraudulent.

By recognizing the threat, Ryan avoided another potential compromise.

As his knowledge expanded, Ryan began helping coworkers improve their own security practices. He shared lessons learned from his experience and encouraged others to adopt proactive defenses. Many were surprised to discover how easily seemingly legitimate software could become a security risk.

Looking back, Ryan realized the spyware incident had ultimately produced a positive outcome. It transformed his perspective on cybersecurity. Instead of assuming security was someone else's responsibility, he recognized that every user plays a role in protecting their own devices and information.

The most valuable lesson he learned was that awareness remains one of the strongest security tools available. Technology can provide protection, but informed decision-making determines how effectively that protection is used.

Today, Ryan still relies heavily on mobile technology. He conducts business, manages finances, communicates with family, and accesses important information through his smartphone. The difference is that he now approaches technology with greater awareness and discipline.

His device remains a powerful tool rather than a vulnerability because he understands that cybersecurity is not a one-time task. It is an ongoing process of observation, education, adaptation, and improvement.

In a world where malware and spyware continue evolving, that mindset became his greatest defense. Through knowledge, vigilance, and preparation, he transformed a potentially damaging experience into the foundation of a stronger and more resilient digital future.

Chapter 5

Creating a Complete Mobile Cybersecurity Defense Plan for Life

Cybersecurity is often viewed as a collection of isolated actions. People install antivirus software, create passwords, enable security settings, or occasionally update their devices. While these individual actions are important, advanced mobile cybersecurity requires a more comprehensive approach. True digital protection comes from developing a long-term defense plan that integrates security into daily life. The most secure individuals are not necessarily those who use the most advanced technology. They are those who consistently follow effective security habits and maintain a proactive mindset.

A cybersecurity defense plan is similar to a personal health plan. Good health is not achieved through a single workout or healthy meal. Instead, it results from consistent behaviors repeated over time. Cybersecurity works the same way. Strong protection develops through regular maintenance, informed decision-making, continuous learning, and disciplined habits. A single security tool cannot eliminate all risks, but a well-designed system can significantly reduce exposure to threats.

The first component of a complete defense plan is asset identification. Before protecting information, users must understand what they are protecting. Smartphones often contain financial information, photographs, business documents, medical records, passwords, private conversations, contact lists, cloud storage access, and social media accounts. Every asset has value. Some assets may be valuable to criminals seeking financial gain. Others may be valuable to advertisers, data brokers, competitors, or malicious individuals. Understanding the importance of these assets helps prioritize protection efforts.

Risk assessment is the second critical component. Not every threat affects every person equally. A business executive may face different risks than a student. A journalist may face different concerns than a retiree. A parent may prioritize family safety, while an entrepreneur may focus on protecting business information. Effective cybersecurity begins by identifying the most relevant threats and allocating resources accordingly.

Once risks have been identified, users should establish layered security controls. Layered security, often referred to as defense in depth, involves creating multiple barriers against attack. If one defense fails, additional layers continue providing protection. For example, a strong password protects an account. Multi-factor authentication adds another layer. Account monitoring provides additional detection capabilities. Together, these controls create a stronger security posture than any single measure alone.

Device security forms the foundation of the defense plan. Smartphones should always be protected by strong authentication methods such as passcodes, fingerprints, or facial recognition. Automatic locking should be enabled to reduce exposure if the device is lost or stolen. Operating systems should remain updated to ensure known vulnerabilities are patched promptly.

Application management is equally important. Users should regularly review installed software and remove applications that are no longer needed. Every application increases the attack surface of the device. Fewer applications generally mean fewer opportunities for exploitation. Permissions should also be reviewed periodically to ensure apps access only the information necessary for their intended functions.

Account security requires ongoing attention. Passwords should be unique for every service. Password managers help simplify credential management while improving security. Multi-factor authentication should be enabled wherever available, especially for financial institutions, email accounts, cloud storage platforms, and social media services.

Backup planning represents another essential component of long-term cybersecurity. Hardware failures, theft, accidental deletion, malware infections, and natural disasters can all result in data loss. Regular backups ensure valuable information remains recoverable. Backups should be tested periodically to confirm they function properly and can be restored when needed.

Monitoring plays a critical role in modern cybersecurity. Prevention is important, but early detection often determines how much damage occurs during a security incident. Users should regularly review account activity, financial statements, login notifications, and device behavior. Unexpected changes should be investigated promptly rather than ignored.

Privacy management should also be incorporated into the defense plan. Many users focus exclusively on security while overlooking privacy concerns. Applications, websites, advertising networks, and data brokers continuously collect information about user behavior. Reviewing privacy settings, limiting permissions, controlling data sharing, and reducing unnecessary exposure help maintain greater control over personal information.

Cybersecurity education is another key element of long-term protection. Threats evolve continuously. New scams, vulnerabilities, attack techniques, and technologies emerge every year. Users who stop learning eventually fall behind. Staying informed through reputable security resources helps individuals recognize emerging risks before they become victims.

Incident response planning is often neglected until it becomes urgently needed. Every user should have a basic response strategy prepared in advance. This plan should include steps for handling lost devices, compromised accounts, malware infections, identity theft incidents, and unauthorized financial activity. Preparing before an emergency improves decision-making and reduces stress during actual incidents.

Physical security remains relevant even in a digital world. Devices should not be left unattended in public locations. Charging stations should be used cautiously. Sensitive information should not be displayed unnecessarily. Travelers should pay special attention to physical device protection because theft often provides attackers with opportunities for compromise.

Family cybersecurity planning is increasingly important as more devices enter homes. Parents should educate children about online safety, privacy protection, social engineering, and responsible technology use. Family members should understand basic security principles and know how to report suspicious activity. A single vulnerable device can create risks for an entire household.

One of the most important concepts in cybersecurity is resilience. Perfect security does not exist. Even highly secure systems occasionally experience incidents. Resilience focuses on recovery and adaptation. Users should expect challenges and prepare to respond effectively. Strong backups, monitoring systems, recovery procedures, and support networks contribute to resilience.

Digital minimalism can further strengthen security. Every online account, connected service, installed application, and shared data point creates potential risk. Reducing unnecessary complexity decreases exposure. Users should periodically review their digital lives and eliminate services that no longer provide value.

As technology continues evolving, artificial intelligence, connected devices, wearable technology, smart homes, and cloud services will create new opportunities and new risks. Cybersecurity defense plans must remain flexible and adaptable. Users should periodically reassess their environments and adjust protections accordingly.

The ultimate goal of a mobile cybersecurity defense plan is not fear or isolation. Technology provides tremendous benefits. Smartphones connect people, enable businesses, facilitate education, provide entertainment, and support countless daily activities. Effective cybersecurity allows users to enjoy these benefits confidently while reducing unnecessary risk.

Security is not a destination. It is a lifelong practice. Every update installed, password strengthened, permission reviewed, backup completed, and suspicious message avoided contributes to a stronger security posture. Small actions performed consistently over time create substantial protection. By adopting a proactive mindset and maintaining a comprehensive defense plan, users can navigate the digital world with greater confidence, awareness, and resilience.

Marcus asked a simple question

Sophia had spent years building her life around technology. Her smartphone managed appointments, banking transactions, work communications, family photos, travel reservations, medical information, and social connections. Like many people, she depended on her device throughout the day without fully appreciating how much of her life it contained.

Over the years, Sophia experienced several minor cybersecurity incidents. A social media account had been compromised. A credit card number had been stolen during a data breach. A phishing email nearly tricked her into revealing account information. None of these events caused catastrophic damage, but together they left her feeling increasingly concerned.

One evening, after receiving another suspicious login alert, Sophia decided it was time to take cybersecurity seriously. Rather than addressing problems individually, she wanted a complete strategy. She contacted Marcus, a cybersecurity consultant known for helping individuals develop long-term security plans.

During their first meeting, Marcus asked a simple question.

"What are you trying to protect?"

Sophia initially struggled to answer. She thought about money, passwords, and devices. Marcus encouraged her to think more broadly. Together, they created a detailed inventory of her digital assets. The list included financial accounts, personal photographs, work documents, health information, cloud storage, social media profiles, email accounts, and family communications.

Seeing everything organized on paper was eye-opening. She realized that cybersecurity was not merely about protecting a smartphone. It was about protecting her entire digital life.

Next, Marcus guided her through a risk assessment. He explained that effective security depends on understanding which threats are most relevant. Sophia was not a celebrity or government official, but she still faced risks from identity theft, phishing attacks, account compromises, malware, and data breaches.

Based on these risks, they developed a layered defense strategy. Passwords were updated and stored within a password manager. Multi-factor authentication was enabled across important services. Backup systems were configured and tested. Privacy settings were reviewed. Device software was updated.

The process took time, but each improvement increased Sophia's confidence.

Several months later, a coworker became the victim of a ransomware attack. Important files were encrypted, and the attacker demanded payment for their release. Watching the situation unfold reinforced the value of her backup strategy. Even if a similar incident occurred, her data could be restored without paying criminals.

Another lesson came during a family vacation. While traveling through a busy airport, Sophia noticed how many people connected to public Wi-Fi networks without hesitation. Because of her training, she understood the potential risks. She avoided conducting sensitive transactions until she returned to trusted networks.

The trip also highlighted the importance of physical security. At one point, she accidentally left her phone on a restaurant table. Fortunately, the device was protected by strong authentication settings. Although she recovered it quickly, the incident reminded her that cybersecurity includes physical protection as well as digital safeguards.

As months turned into years, cybersecurity became part of Sophia's routine. She no longer viewed security tasks as burdensome chores. They became normal habits, much like locking doors, wearing seat belts, or maintaining insurance coverage.

She scheduled regular security reviews every few months. During these reviews, she updated passwords, checked account activity, reviewed permissions, and assessed any changes in her technology use. These small investments of time provided ongoing peace of mind.

One day, Sophia received a highly sophisticated phishing email. The message appeared to come from a trusted financial institution. The branding was professional. The language was convincing. The request seemed reasonable.

Yet something felt slightly unusual.

Instead of responding immediately, Sophia verified the request through official channels. Her suspicion proved correct. The message was fraudulent.

Years earlier, she likely would have fallen victim to the scam. Now, her awareness protected her.

Eventually, friends and family began asking for advice. Sophia shared the principles she had learned from Marcus. She explained that cybersecurity is not about becoming an expert hacker or purchasing expensive software. It is about developing consistent habits and maintaining awareness.

Her teenage son benefited particularly from these lessons. By teaching him about privacy, authentication, phishing, and responsible technology use, she helped him develop strong security practices early in life. The knowledge became a valuable skill he would carry into adulthood.

Looking back, Sophia realized the most important change was not technical. It was psychological. She no longer felt powerless in the face of cyber threats. She understood the risks, implemented practical defenses, and prepared for potential incidents.

Technology continued evolving around her. New devices appeared. New applications emerged. New threats entered the cybersecurity landscape. Yet the principles underlying her defense plan remained effective because they were based on awareness, preparation, and adaptability.

Sophia understood that cybersecurity would never be completely finished. There would always be updates to install, threats to monitor, and lessons to learn. Rather than viewing this reality as exhausting, she viewed it as empowering.

Her defense plan provided structure. Her habits provided consistency. Her knowledge provided confidence.

Most importantly, she recognized that cybersecurity was not about living in fear. It was about maintaining control. Through thoughtful planning, informed decisions, and ongoing vigilance, she had created a secure digital environment that allowed her to enjoy the benefits of technology while minimizing unnecessary risk.

That balance—between convenience and protection, innovation and caution, opportunity and responsibility—became the foundation of her digital life. It was a lesson she hoped future generations would embrace as technology continued shaping the world around them.

Chapter 6

The Future of Mobile Cybersecurity and Becoming Your Own Digital Defender

The world of mobile cybersecurity is constantly evolving. The threats that existed ten years ago differ significantly from those encountered today, and the threats of tomorrow will continue changing as technology advances. Mobile devices have transformed from simple communication tools into powerful computing platforms that manage finances, healthcare information, business operations, personal relationships, entertainment, education, and countless other aspects of daily life. As mobile technology becomes more deeply integrated into society, the importance of cybersecurity will continue to grow.

Understanding future cybersecurity challenges requires recognizing a fundamental reality: attackers and defenders are engaged in a continuous cycle of adaptation. Every new security control eventually inspires new attack methods. Every new attack technique leads to new defensive strategies. This ongoing competition drives innovation on both sides. Individuals who understand this dynamic are better prepared to adapt to changing threats.

Artificial intelligence is expected to play a major role in the future of mobile cybersecurity. AI technologies are already helping organizations identify suspicious behavior, detect malware, analyze network activity, and automate security monitoring. These capabilities allow defenders to respond more quickly to threats and identify patterns that might otherwise go unnoticed. As AI systems continue improving, they will likely become even more effective at detecting and preventing cyberattacks.

However, artificial intelligence also creates opportunities for attackers. Cybercriminals increasingly use AI tools to automate phishing campaigns, generate convincing fraudulent messages, create realistic fake voices, and identify vulnerabilities more efficiently. Attackers can now produce personalized scams at a scale previously impossible. Understanding these developments is essential because future cyber threats may become increasingly sophisticated and difficult to recognize.

Deepfake technology presents another emerging challenge. Advances in audio and video generation make it possible to create highly convincing fake content. Attackers may use deepfakes to impersonate executives, family members, public figures, or trusted contacts. Mobile users should become accustomed to verifying unusual requests through multiple channels rather than relying solely on voice or video evidence.

The expansion of connected devices will also influence mobile cybersecurity. Smartphones increasingly serve as central control hubs for smart homes, vehicles, wearable devices, healthcare equipment, and Internet of Things (IoT) technologies. Every connected device introduces additional opportunities for attackers. Securing a smartphone may no longer be sufficient if other connected devices remain vulnerable.

Cloud computing continues transforming how information is stored and accessed. Rather than maintaining files exclusively on local devices, users increasingly rely on cloud services for storage, collaboration, backups, and communication. While cloud technologies provide convenience and resilience, they also require careful attention to account security, authentication practices, and access controls.

Biometric authentication will likely become more advanced in coming years. Fingerprints, facial recognition systems, behavioral analysis, voice authentication, and other identification methods may continue improving. These technologies can enhance both convenience and security, but users should remember that no single authentication method is infallible. Layered security remains important regardless of technological advances.

Privacy concerns are expected to remain significant. Data collection continues expanding across applications, devices, platforms, and services. Governments, corporations, advertisers, and other organizations increasingly rely on data analytics to make decisions and generate insights. Users who value privacy must remain informed about how information is collected, stored, shared, and protected.

Regulatory changes may influence future cybersecurity practices. Governments worldwide are introducing laws designed to improve data protection, strengthen privacy rights, and increase organizational accountability. While regulations can provide important safeguards, individuals should not assume that laws alone will eliminate cyber risks. Personal responsibility remains an essential component of digital security.

Cybersecurity education will become increasingly valuable as technology evolves. Technical defenses are important, but informed decision-making often determines whether attacks succeed. Attackers frequently exploit human psychology through social engineering, deception, urgency, and manipulation. Understanding these tactics allows individuals to recognize threats before becoming victims.

The concept of digital resilience is likely to become even more important in the future. Traditional cybersecurity often focuses on prevention, but resilience emphasizes preparation, recovery, and adaptation. Because no system can guarantee complete protection, users should prepare for the possibility of incidents and develop strategies for responding effectively.

Developing a security mindset represents one of the most valuable long-term investments individuals can make. A security mindset involves questioning unexpected requests, verifying information before acting, considering potential risks, and evaluating how decisions may affect security. This mindset applies across technologies, platforms, and environments.

One common mistake is assuming cybersecurity is solely a technical field. In reality, cybersecurity is also a behavioral discipline. Strong habits often provide greater protection than expensive tools. Consistently updating software, reviewing permissions, using strong authentication, maintaining backups, and exercising caution online create substantial security benefits.

Future technologies may introduce entirely new categories of cyber threats. Quantum computing, augmented reality systems, advanced wearable devices, autonomous systems, and emerging communication technologies may create security challenges that are difficult to predict today. Fortunately, the foundational principles of cybersecurity remain remarkably stable despite technological change.

These principles include awareness, preparation, authentication, privacy protection, risk management, monitoring, resilience, and continuous learning. Individuals who master these concepts can adapt to evolving technologies more effectively than those who rely solely on specific tools or techniques.

Perhaps the most important lesson of advanced cybersecurity is that every user plays a role in their own protection. Security professionals, software developers, device manufacturers, and regulatory agencies all contribute to cybersecurity, but individuals remain responsible for many of the decisions that affect their digital safety.

Becoming your own digital defender means taking ownership of security practices. It means understanding threats, implementing defenses, maintaining awareness, and continuously improving. This responsibility may seem significant, but it is also empowering. Knowledge reduces uncertainty. Preparation reduces risk. Awareness increases confidence.

The future will undoubtedly bring new challenges, but it will also provide new opportunities. Technology continues improving lives in countless ways. Mobile devices connect people across the world, provide access to information, support businesses, enable education, and facilitate innovation. Effective cybersecurity allows individuals to embrace these opportunities while protecting themselves from unnecessary harm.

Ultimately, advanced mobile cybersecurity is not about fear, restriction, or avoiding technology. It is about using technology wisely. It is about balancing convenience with security, innovation with caution, and opportunity with responsibility. By developing strong habits, maintaining awareness, and embracing lifelong learning, users can remain secure and resilient in an increasingly connected world.

Ethan began studying emerging technologies more closely

Ethan had always enjoyed technology. As a teenager, he eagerly adopted new devices, experimented with emerging applications, and followed developments in artificial intelligence, cloud computing, and mobile technology. By the time he entered adulthood, his smartphone had become the center of nearly every aspect of his life.

His device managed banking, investments, healthcare records, business communications, travel plans, education, entertainment, and family connections. Like many people, he depended on technology daily but rarely considered what the future might bring from a cybersecurity perspective.

One afternoon, Ethan attended a cybersecurity conference hosted by a local technology organization. Initially, he expected technical presentations focused on malware and hacking. Instead, many speakers discussed broader topics such as artificial intelligence, digital resilience, privacy rights, behavioral security, and the future of connected technologies.

One presentation in particular captured his attention.

The speaker explained that cybersecurity is no longer simply about protecting computers. It is about protecting lives that increasingly depend on digital systems. Smartphones, vehicles, homes, financial institutions, healthcare providers, and communication networks are becoming interconnected. As a result, cybersecurity decisions have real-world consequences.

The presentation challenged Ethan's assumptions. He realized that cybersecurity was not merely a technical skill. It was becoming a life skill.

Inspired by what he learned, Ethan began studying emerging technologies more closely. He followed developments in artificial intelligence and discovered both exciting opportunities and concerning risks. AI tools improved productivity, enhanced security monitoring, and simplified many tasks. At the same time, cybercriminals used similar technologies to create convincing scams and automated attacks.

One day, Ethan received a voicemail from what appeared to be a family member requesting urgent financial assistance. The voice sounded authentic. The situation seemed believable. Yet something felt unusual.

Remembering the conference discussion about deepfake technology, Ethan decided to verify the request directly. He contacted the family member through another communication channel and discovered that the message was fraudulent. The voice had been artificially generated.

The experience reinforced the importance of verification. Technology could no longer be trusted solely based on appearances.

As years passed, Ethan continued developing his cybersecurity knowledge. He adopted a security mindset rather than relying exclusively on tools. Before clicking links, sharing information, granting permissions, or responding to requests, he paused to evaluate potential risks.

His habits extended beyond personal protection. He helped family members secure their devices, taught younger relatives about online safety, and encouraged coworkers to adopt stronger security practices. Rather than viewing cybersecurity as a specialized profession, he viewed it as a shared responsibility.

Several years later, Ethan purchased a smart home system that connected lighting, security cameras, climate controls, and appliances to his smartphone. While the technology offered convenience, he recognized the importance of securing these devices properly. Strong authentication, software updates, network segmentation, and careful configuration became part of his setup process.

Many of his friends focused exclusively on functionality. Ethan considered security from the beginning. As a result, he avoided several common vulnerabilities that affected less-prepared users.

One evening, while reading technology news, Ethan encountered reports describing a major data breach affecting millions of users. Although the incident generated significant media attention, he remained relatively calm. His passwords were unique. Multi-factor authentication was enabled. Monitoring systems alerted him to unusual activity. Backup plans were already established.

He understood that perfect security did not exist. Breaches, attacks, and vulnerabilities would continue occurring. The goal was not eliminating all risk but managing risk effectively.

This perspective proved valuable when one of his online accounts was targeted during a credential-stuffing attack. Because strong authentication measures were already in place, attackers failed to gain access. The incident became a minor inconvenience rather than a major crisis.

Over time, Ethan noticed a significant shift in his relationship with technology. Earlier in life, he often viewed cybersecurity as reactive. Problems occurred first, and solutions followed. Now, cybersecurity was proactive. Preparation occurred before incidents developed.

The change provided peace of mind. Instead of worrying constantly about potential threats, he focused on maintaining good habits and staying informed. Security became part of his routine rather than a source of anxiety.

Years later, Ethan reflected on everything he had learned. Technology had changed dramatically since his youth. Smartphones became more powerful. Artificial intelligence transformed industries. Connected devices became commonplace. Yet the most important cybersecurity lessons remained remarkably consistent.

Awareness mattered.

Preparation mattered.

Verification mattered.

Adaptability mattered.

Continuous learning mattered.

Most importantly, personal responsibility mattered.

Ethan realized that becoming a digital defender was not a destination. It was an ongoing journey. Every year would bring new technologies, new opportunities, and new risks. The individuals most likely to thrive would not necessarily be the most technical. They would be the most adaptable.

By embracing cybersecurity as a lifelong practice rather than a one-time task, Ethan had developed confidence in his ability to navigate an uncertain digital future. He understood that challenges would continue emerging, but he also knew he possessed the knowledge, habits, and mindset necessary to respond effectively.

That confidence became his greatest security asset.

As technology continued reshaping the world, Ethan remained optimistic. He believed innovation and security could coexist. He believed individuals could enjoy the benefits of technology without sacrificing privacy or safety. Most importantly, he believed that informed users had the power to shape their own digital futures.

The future of cybersecurity would undoubtedly evolve, but the role of the digital defender would remain essential. Through awareness, preparation, resilience, and lifelong learning, every individual could become the first and most important line of defense in protecting their digital life.

by embracing cybersecurity as a lifelong practice rather than a one-time task, Lakshmi had developed confidence in his ability to navigate an uncertain digital future. He understood that challenges would continue emerging, but he also knew he possessed the knowledge, habits, and mindset necessary to respond effectively.

That confidence became his greatest security asset.

As technology continued reshaping the world, Pihar remained optimistic. He believed innovation and security could coexist. He believed individuals could enjoy the benefits of technology without sacrificing privacy or safety. Most importantly, he believed that informed users had the power to shape their own digital futures.

The future of cybersecurity would undoubtedly evolve, but the role of the digital defender would remain essential. Through awareness, preparation, resilience, and lifelong learning, every individual could become the first and most important line of defense in protecting their digital life.

Chapter 7

Mastering Lifelong Mobile Security, Digital Freedom, and Cyber Resilience

As we reach the final chapter of this book, it is important to recognize that cybersecurity is not a destination. It is a lifelong journey. Technology will continue evolving, new threats will emerge, and digital systems will become increasingly integrated into everyday life. The most successful mobile users will not necessarily be those with the most advanced devices or the most expensive security software. They will be the individuals who develop strong habits, maintain awareness, adapt to change, and build lasting cyber resilience.

Cyber resilience is one of the most important concepts in modern cybersecurity. Traditional security strategies often focus exclusively on prevention. While prevention remains valuable, no system can guarantee complete protection. Devices can be lost. Accounts can be targeted. Data breaches can occur. New vulnerabilities can appear unexpectedly. Cyber resilience recognizes this reality and emphasizes the ability to prepare, respond, recover, and adapt when incidents occur.

Resilient individuals understand that cybersecurity is not about achieving perfection. It is about reducing risk while maintaining the ability to recover from setbacks. Just as physically healthy individuals may still become ill but recover more effectively, cyber-resilient individuals may encounter security incidents but possess the tools, knowledge, and preparation necessary to minimize damage and restore normal operations.

One of the foundations of cyber resilience is maintaining strong security habits. Habits are powerful because they operate consistently over time. Many people focus intensely on security immediately after experiencing a cyber incident but gradually return to risky behaviors as memories fade. Effective cybersecurity requires long-term discipline. Small actions repeated consistently often provide greater protection than occasional large efforts.

Password management remains a critical habit. Unique credentials, password managers, and multi-factor authentication continue providing substantial protection regardless of how technology evolves. These practices represent foundational defenses that remain effective across platforms, devices, and services. As new technologies emerge, strong authentication will continue serving as a cornerstone of security.

Software maintenance is another essential habit. Updates are frequently viewed as inconvenient interruptions, yet they play a critical role in reducing vulnerability exposure. Developers continuously identify and fix weaknesses that attackers may attempt to exploit. Promptly applying updates significantly reduces risk and improves device security.

Digital awareness represents an equally important skill. Awareness involves understanding how technology works, recognizing potential threats, and evaluating situations before taking action. Many cyberattacks succeed because individuals react emotionally rather than thoughtfully. Fear, urgency, curiosity, excitement, and trust are frequently exploited by attackers. Developing awareness helps users recognize manipulation attempts before becoming victims.

Information verification has become increasingly important in an era of misinformation, deepfakes, artificial intelligence, and sophisticated social engineering attacks. Users should verify unusual requests, confirm financial transactions, validate communications, and seek independent confirmation when circumstances appear suspicious. Verification often prevents incidents that technology alone cannot stop.

Privacy protection remains closely connected to long-term security. Excessive information sharing increases exposure to risks such as identity theft, fraud, surveillance, and social engineering attacks. Users should regularly evaluate what information they share, who has access to it, and whether that sharing remains necessary. Privacy management is not about secrecy; it is about maintaining appropriate control over personal information.

Financial security deserves special attention within a comprehensive cybersecurity strategy. Mobile devices increasingly serve as gateways to banking services, investment platforms, payment systems, and digital assets. Monitoring financial accounts regularly helps identify suspicious activity early. Alerts, transaction notifications, and account reviews contribute to stronger financial protection.

Emotional resilience is another often-overlooked aspect of cybersecurity. Cyber incidents can create stress, anxiety, frustration, and fear. Individuals who remain calm during security events generally make better decisions than those who panic. Preparing response plans in advance helps reduce uncertainty and supports rational decision-making during incidents.

Continuous learning is essential because cybersecurity is constantly changing. Attack techniques evolve. Technologies improve. Regulations change. New risks emerge. Lifelong learners remain better equipped to recognize threats and adapt their defenses. Reading security news, attending educational events, participating in training programs, and following reputable experts help maintain awareness.

One powerful strategy for long-term success is conducting periodic security reviews. These reviews provide opportunities to assess current protections, identify weaknesses, and implement improvements. Users should evaluate passwords, account security settings, installed applications, backups, privacy controls, and device configurations on a regular basis.

The principle of digital minimalism can significantly improve cybersecurity. Many users accumulate accounts, applications, subscriptions, and connected services over time. Each additional component introduces potential risk. Removing unnecessary accounts, uninstalling unused software, and simplifying digital environments often improves both security and privacy.

Community support also contributes to resilience. Family members, friends, coworkers, and professional advisors can provide valuable assistance during cybersecurity incidents. Sharing knowledge and encouraging safe practices help strengthen collective security. Cybersecurity should not be viewed solely as an individual responsibility. Strong communities create stronger defenses.

As technology becomes increasingly integrated into daily life, cybersecurity will influence nearly every area of society. Education, healthcare, transportation, finance, government, communication, and entertainment all depend upon secure digital systems. Individuals who understand cybersecurity principles will be better prepared to navigate this environment confidently and responsibly.

One of the most empowering aspects of cybersecurity is recognizing that users possess significant control over their own protection. Threats may exist, but so do effective defenses. Attackers may develop new techniques, but awareness and preparation remain powerful countermeasures. Knowledge transforms uncertainty into confidence and vulnerability into resilience.

Digital freedom emerges when individuals understand how technology works and make informed choices regarding its use. Freedom does not mean ignoring risks. Instead, it means engaging with technology confidently while maintaining appropriate safeguards. Security enables freedom by reducing fear and increasing trust in the systems people depend upon every day.

Throughout this book, numerous topics have been explored, including authentication, privacy protection, malware defense, surveillance awareness, identity theft prevention, incident response, security planning, and future cybersecurity trends. Although each topic is important individually, their greatest value emerges when combined into a comprehensive security mindset.

This mindset recognizes that cybersecurity is not a product that can be purchased or a setting that can be enabled once and forgotten. It is a process. It is a way of thinking. It is a commitment to awareness, preparation, responsibility, and continuous improvement.

The future will undoubtedly bring challenges. New technologies will create new risks. Cybercriminals will continue adapting. Yet individuals who develop strong habits, maintain resilience, embrace learning, and take responsibility for their digital lives will be well-positioned to thrive.

The goal is not perfection.

The goal is preparedness.

The goal is resilience.

The goal is maintaining control over your digital life while enjoying the benefits that technology provides.

By adopting these principles and practicing them consistently, you can build a foundation of security that supports personal growth, professional success, financial stability, privacy protection, and long-term peace of mind.

Olivia attended a community technology workshop

When Olivia purchased her first smartphone many years ago, she viewed it as a simple communication device. She used it for calls, text messages, and occasional internet browsing. Over time, however, the device became far more important. It evolved into a digital wallet, personal assistant, navigation system, camera, office, entertainment center, health tracker, and gateway to nearly every aspect of modern life.

As technology became more central to her daily routine, Olivia experienced both the benefits and risks of the digital world. She encountered phishing attempts, fraudulent messages, suspicious applications, and privacy concerns. Fortunately, most incidents were minor, but each one taught valuable lessons about the importance of cybersecurity.

One evening, while organizing old photographs, Olivia reflected on how much technology had changed during her lifetime. The transformation was remarkable. Yet she realized that her understanding of security had evolved just as dramatically.

Years earlier, she viewed cybersecurity as something handled by technology companies and security experts. If problems occurred, she expected someone else to solve them. Over time, she learned that individual actions play a crucial role in digital safety.

This realization began several years earlier when a close friend became the victim of identity theft. The recovery process lasted months and involved financial institutions, credit bureaus, law enforcement agencies, and numerous account providers. Watching the experience unfold motivated Olivia to strengthen her own security practices.

She started with simple improvements. Passwords became stronger and unique. Multi-factor authentication was enabled. Backups were configured. Privacy settings were reviewed. Software updates were installed promptly.

Initially, these tasks felt inconvenient.

Eventually, they became habits.

As the years passed, Olivia encountered additional challenges. A data breach exposed information from one of her online accounts. A phishing email targeted her workplace. A family member accidentally installed a suspicious application. Yet each situation reinforced the value of preparation.

Because strong passwords were already in place, the data breach caused minimal disruption.

Because she understood phishing techniques, the fraudulent email failed.

Because her family discussed cybersecurity openly, the suspicious application was identified and removed quickly.

Each incident demonstrated an important principle. Preparation before an event is far more effective than reacting afterward.

One summer, Olivia attended a community technology workshop focused on digital literacy. The instructor discussed cyber resilience and explained that no one can prevent every possible incident. Instead, the goal is developing the ability to recover and adapt.

The concept resonated deeply.

She realized that resilience applied to many areas of life. Financial resilience helps people overcome economic setbacks. Physical resilience supports recovery from illness or injury. Emotional resilience helps individuals navigate adversity. Cyber resilience performs a similar function within the digital world.

This perspective changed how she approached security.

Rather than seeking perfect protection, she focused on creating strong systems and healthy habits. Backups were maintained. Security reviews were scheduled. Important documents were organized. Recovery procedures were documented. Family members understood how to respond if problems occurred.

Several years later, those preparations proved valuable when her smartphone was stolen during a crowded public event.

Initially, the situation was stressful.

However, instead of panicking, Olivia followed her response plan. The device was remotely locked. Account credentials were updated. Tracking features were activated. Financial accounts were monitored. A replacement device was configured using existing backups.

Within days, normal operations resumed.

The incident reinforced her confidence. Although losing the device was inconvenient, it did not become a disaster because preparation had reduced its impact.

As technology continued evolving, Olivia remained committed to learning. She followed developments in artificial intelligence, privacy regulations, authentication technologies, and emerging cyber threats. Rather than fearing change, she embraced education as a tool for adaptation.

Her curiosity eventually inspired others. Friends frequently asked for advice. Family members sought help securing devices and accounts. Younger relatives learned about online safety from her experiences. Without realizing it, Olivia had become a cybersecurity advocate within her community.

One conversation stood out particularly.

A teenager asked whether cybersecurity was difficult to learn.

Olivia smiled and replied that cybersecurity is not primarily about computers. It is about habits, awareness, and decision-making.

Technology changes.

Principles endure.

That simple statement captured everything she had learned throughout her journey.

Years later, while reviewing old journals, Olivia discovered notes describing her early experiences with smartphones. Reading those entries reminded her how much confidence she had gained. Technology no longer felt mysterious or intimidating. She understood how to use it safely, how to recognize risks, and how to respond when challenges appeared.

Most importantly, she understood that cybersecurity was not about living in fear.

It was about living with confidence.

By developing knowledge, maintaining awareness, and practicing resilience, she had created a secure digital foundation that supported every aspect of her life.

As she looked toward the future, Olivia knew new technologies and new threats would continue emerging. Yet she felt prepared. Not because she possessed perfect knowledge or flawless defenses, but because she had developed the mindset necessary to adapt.

That mindset—built upon awareness, responsibility, resilience, and lifelong learning—became her greatest cybersecurity asset.

And in a world where digital systems increasingly influence every aspect of life, it was a gift that would continue serving her for years to come.

intimidating. She understood how to use it safely, how to recognize risks, and how to respond when challenges appeared.

Most importantly, she understood that cybersecurity was not about living in fear.

It was about living with confidence.

By developing knowledge, maintaining awareness, and practicing resilience, she had created a secure digital foundation that supported every aspect of her life.

As she looked toward the future, Olivia knew new technologies and new threats would continue emerging. Yet she felt prepared. Not because she possessed perfect knowledge or flawless defenses, but because she had developed the mindset necessary to adapt.

That mindset—built upon awareness, responsibility, resilience, and lifelong learning—became her greatest cybersecurity asset.

And in a world where digital systems increasingly influence every aspect of life, it was a gift that would continue serving her for years to come.

Chapter 8

Building Your Personal Cybersecurity Legacy and Thriving in the Digital Age

As we conclude this journey through advanced mobile cybersecurity and digital defense, it is important to shift our focus from individual security practices to a broader and more enduring concept: creating a personal cybersecurity legacy. A cybersecurity legacy is the collection of habits, knowledge, systems, values, and behaviors that continue protecting you, your family, your business, and future generations long after individual devices, applications, and technologies have changed.

Many people view cybersecurity as a temporary concern tied to current technology. They focus on protecting a specific smartphone, securing a particular account, or responding to a recent threat. While these actions are important, long-term success comes from developing principles that remain effective regardless of technological change. Devices will evolve. Operating systems will change. Applications will come and go. Yet the principles of awareness, preparation, responsibility, and resilience remain timeless.

One of the most important aspects of building a cybersecurity legacy is recognizing that security knowledge compounds over time. Every lesson learned strengthens future decision-making. Every security habit reduces future risk. Every conversation about digital safety contributes to a more secure environment. Just as financial investments grow through consistent contributions, cybersecurity benefits accumulate through continuous effort and learning.

The digital world has become deeply interconnected. A security weakness affecting one individual can create risks for family members, coworkers, organizations, and communities. This interconnected reality means that personal cybersecurity decisions have broader consequences. By maintaining strong security practices, individuals contribute to collective security and help create safer digital environments for others.

Education remains one of the most valuable cybersecurity investments available. Technologies change rapidly, but educated individuals adapt more effectively than those who rely solely on tools or specific products. Understanding how attackers think, how systems operate, and how risks emerge enables users to make informed decisions regardless of changing circumstances.

A cybersecurity legacy begins with personal responsibility. Rather than expecting software companies, governments, employers, or security professionals to provide complete protection, resilient individuals recognize their own role in managing risk. They understand that technology can support security, but informed decisions ultimately determine outcomes.

One essential component of a lasting cybersecurity strategy is documentation. Important account information, emergency procedures, recovery plans, backup locations, and security contacts should be organized and maintained securely. Many individuals spend years building digital assets without creating plans for managing them during emergencies. Proper documentation improves resilience and ensures continuity when unexpected events occur.

Digital estate planning has become increasingly important. Individuals now possess significant digital assets, including photographs, documents, financial accounts, online businesses, cloud storage, cryptocurrencies, social media profiles, and intellectual property. Planning for the management and transfer of these assets helps protect their value and reduces complications for family members.

Families should develop shared cybersecurity practices. Household members often use connected devices, shared networks, streaming services, smart home systems, and communication platforms. Establishing common security standards improves protection for everyone involved. Family discussions about online safety, privacy, scams, and responsible technology use create awareness that extends across generations.

Business owners face additional responsibilities. Mobile devices increasingly serve as gateways to customer information, financial systems, communication platforms, and operational data. Strong cybersecurity practices protect not only the business owner but also clients, partners, and employees. Even small businesses benefit significantly from implementing structured security programs.

One of the most effective ways to strengthen long-term security is through routine. Security should not depend upon memory or motivation alone. Establishing recurring reviews, scheduled updates, backup procedures, password audits, and account monitoring activities helps ensure consistency. When security becomes routine, it requires less effort and delivers greater benefits.

Adaptability represents another critical element of cybersecurity success. Technology evolves continuously. New devices, services, threats, and opportunities emerge every year. Individuals who remain flexible and open to learning are better positioned to respond effectively. Adaptability reduces fear because it creates confidence in one's ability to navigate uncertainty.

The concept of digital citizenship also deserves attention. Responsible technology use extends beyond personal protection. Ethical online behavior, respect for privacy, accurate information sharing, and support for secure practices contribute to healthier digital communities. Strong cybersecurity cultures emerge when individuals take responsibility for both their own actions and their impact on others.

Cybersecurity leadership is not limited to professionals working in technical fields. Anyone can become a leader by modeling good habits, sharing knowledge, encouraging safe practices, and helping others navigate digital risks. Informal leadership often influences behavior more effectively than formal policies or regulations.

As artificial intelligence, automation, wearable devices, virtual reality systems, smart cities, and other technologies continue developing, cybersecurity will become increasingly integrated into daily life. Security considerations will influence healthcare, education, transportation, finance, communication, and entertainment. Individuals who understand cybersecurity principles will possess valuable skills applicable across numerous domains.

Confidence plays an important role in cybersecurity. Many people feel overwhelmed by technical terminology and rapidly changing threats. However, effective cybersecurity does not require advanced technical expertise. It requires awareness, curiosity, discipline, and a willingness to learn. Confidence grows through experience, education, and preparation.

One common misconception is that cybersecurity focuses exclusively on avoiding negative outcomes. In reality, strong cybersecurity enables positive opportunities. Secure individuals can conduct business online with greater confidence, explore new technologies more comfortably, communicate more freely, and participate more fully in the digital economy. Security creates freedom by reducing uncertainty.

The future of mobile technology promises extraordinary possibilities. Artificial intelligence assistants, advanced healthcare monitoring, immersive communication tools, autonomous systems, and innovative financial technologies will continue transforming daily life. Embracing these opportunities responsibly requires balancing innovation with security.

Ultimately, a cybersecurity legacy is not measured by the number of security tools used or technical certifications earned. It is measured by the habits established, the knowledge shared, the resilience developed, and the positive impact created. A strong cybersecurity legacy protects individuals today while preparing future generations for tomorrow's challenges.

The digital age will continue evolving, but individuals who embrace lifelong learning, maintain awareness, practice responsibility, and cultivate resilience will remain well-equipped to thrive. Cybersecurity is not merely about defending against threats. It is about creating a foundation that supports opportunity, freedom, confidence, and long-term success.

He discovered that effective cybersecurity depended less on technical complexity and more on consistent habits

Michael never expected cybersecurity to become one of the most valuable skills he would develop during his lifetime.

When he purchased his first smartphone many years earlier, he viewed technology primarily as a convenience. It helped him communicate, navigate unfamiliar places, manage appointments, and access information quickly. Like many people, he appreciated the benefits without thinking much about security.

Over time, technology became increasingly important. His smartphone connected him to financial institutions, healthcare providers, business partners, friends, family members, and countless online services. Gradually, he realized that much of his life existed in digital form.

His cybersecurity journey began after a minor incident involving a compromised social media account. The event caused little lasting damage, but it sparked curiosity. Michael started reading about online security, identity protection, privacy management, and digital resilience.

At first, the information seemed overwhelming. There were countless threats, recommendations, tools, and opinions. However, as he continued learning, he discovered that effective cybersecurity depended less on technical complexity and more on consistent habits.

He strengthened passwords.

He enabled multi-factor authentication.

He reviewed privacy settings.

He organized backups.

He stayed informed.

These simple actions gradually became part of his routine.

Years later, Michael owned a successful consulting business that relied heavily on mobile technology. Client communications, project files, financial records, and operational systems all depended upon secure digital infrastructure. The habits he developed personally now benefited his professional life as well.

One day, a younger employee named Daniel approached him with concerns about cybersecurity. Daniel had recently fallen victim to a phishing attempt and felt embarrassed by the experience.

Rather than criticizing him, Michael shared his own story.

He explained that cybersecurity is a journey rather than a destination. Everyone makes mistakes. What matters is learning from those experiences and improving over time.

The conversation had a profound impact on Daniel. Inspired by Michael's perspective, he began strengthening his own security practices. Eventually, he helped other employees improve theirs as well.

Michael realized that cybersecurity knowledge becomes more valuable when shared.

As the years passed, he extended these conversations beyond the workplace. He discussed online safety with family members. He helped aging relatives recognize scams. He taught children about privacy and responsible technology use. Each discussion contributed to a stronger security culture within his community.

One holiday gathering highlighted the importance of these efforts.

Several family members shared stories about fraudulent messages, suspicious phone calls, and attempted scams. Because they had previously discussed cybersecurity together, many recognized warning signs and avoided becoming victims.

Listening to these stories, Michael understood something important.

Cybersecurity was no longer merely a personal concern.

It had become a family asset.

The knowledge passed from one person to another created protection that extended far beyond any individual device or account.

As technology advanced, Michael remained committed to learning. Artificial intelligence transformed communication. Smart devices became commonplace. New forms of digital identity emerged. Yet the principles that guided his decisions remained remarkably consistent.

Stay informed.

Verify information.

Protect privacy.

Prepare for incidents.

Continue learning.

Help others.

These principles provided stability even as technologies changed.

Several years later, Michael began organizing his digital assets more intentionally. He documented account information, created recovery plans, secured important records, and established procedures that would assist family members if emergencies occurred. This process introduced him to the concept of a cybersecurity legacy.

The idea resonated deeply.

Just as people create financial plans, educational plans, and estate plans, they should also create digital protection plans. Future generations would inherit not only assets but also digital responsibilities. Preparing them in advance would reduce confusion and improve resilience.

One evening, while reviewing family photographs stored in the cloud, Michael reflected on how much technology had changed throughout his lifetime. The devices were different. The applications were different. The threats were different.

Yet one thing remained constant.

Technology was most beneficial when used thoughtfully and responsibly.

Years later, after retiring from full-time consulting, Michael continued mentoring younger professionals and community members. Many sought technical advice, but he often focused on something simpler.

Mindset.

Tools would change.

Threats would evolve.

Platforms would disappear.

But a strong cybersecurity mindset would remain valuable indefinitely.

The ability to think critically, adapt to change, verify information, and manage risk would serve individuals throughout their lives.

As he looked toward the future, Michael felt optimistic. New technologies would undoubtedly create new challenges, but they would also create extraordinary opportunities. Individuals prepared to navigate those opportunities responsibly would benefit enormously.

His greatest satisfaction came not from the devices he used or the accounts he protected. It came from knowing that the habits, knowledge, and values he shared would continue helping others long after specific technologies became obsolete.

That was his cybersecurity legacy.

Not a collection of passwords.

Not a set of software tools.

Not a technical achievement.

A legacy of awareness.

A legacy of resilience.

A legacy of responsibility.

A legacy of confidence.

And in a world increasingly shaped by technology, it was one of the most valuable gifts he could leave behind.

Chapter 9

The Mobile Cybersecurity Master Plan – Integrating Everything Into One Complete Defense System

Throughout this book and the entire Mobile Security & App Protection Academy series, you have explored numerous aspects of cybersecurity. You have learned about device security, privacy protection, application security, authentication systems, malware defense, identity theft prevention, digital resilience, future technologies, and long-term cybersecurity planning. Each of these topics provides important value individually. However, true cybersecurity mastery comes from understanding how all these components work together as part of a complete defense system.

Many individuals make the mistake of treating cybersecurity as a collection of separate tasks. They focus on passwords one month, software updates another month, and privacy settings only after reading about a data breach. While these efforts help, they often lack coordination. A more effective approach involves creating a unified security strategy where every layer supports the others.

The concept of a cybersecurity master plan is based on integration. Every defensive measure should contribute to an overall system designed to protect personal information, financial assets, digital identities, communications, devices, and future opportunities. Security becomes significantly stronger when individual components reinforce one another.

The foundation of every cybersecurity master plan is awareness. Awareness serves as the first line of defense because most attacks begin with human interaction. Attackers frequently rely on deception rather than technical sophistication. Phishing emails, fraudulent text messages, fake applications, social engineering schemes, and online scams all depend upon convincing users to take actions that compromise security. Awareness disrupts these attacks before they succeed.

The second layer of the master plan involves device protection. Smartphones and tablets function as gateways to critical information and services. Securing these devices through strong authentication, encryption, software updates, and secure configurations helps reduce vulnerability exposure. Devices should be viewed as valuable assets deserving ongoing protection.

The third layer focuses on identity protection. Digital identities now influence financial services, employment opportunities, healthcare access, communication systems, and countless other activities. Protecting identities requires strong passwords, password managers, multi-factor authentication, account monitoring, and cautious information sharing. Identity security forms one of the most important aspects of long-term digital protection.

The fourth layer addresses privacy management. Every application, website, platform, and connected service collects information. Users should understand what information is being gathered, how it is used, and whether sharing remains necessary. Privacy controls help reduce unnecessary exposure and provide greater control over personal information.

The fifth layer consists of application security. Every installed application introduces potential risk. Applications should be reviewed carefully before installation, permissions should be evaluated regularly, and unused software should be removed. A smaller attack surface generally improves security outcomes.

The sixth layer focuses on communication security. Messages, emails, phone calls, video conferences, and social media interactions often contain sensitive information. Secure communication practices include verifying contacts, using encrypted services when appropriate, recognizing phishing attempts, and avoiding unnecessary information disclosure.

The seventh layer addresses financial security. Mobile devices increasingly facilitate banking, investing, shopping, and payment processing. Financial security requires transaction monitoring, account alerts, secure payment practices, identity theft prevention measures, and rapid response procedures for suspicious activity.

The eighth layer involves backup and recovery planning. Every cybersecurity strategy should assume that incidents may occur despite preventive efforts. Backups preserve important information, while recovery plans help restore operations efficiently. Together, they contribute significantly to resilience.

The ninth layer focuses on monitoring and maintenance. Security is not a one-time project. It requires continuous attention. Accounts should be reviewed regularly. Devices should be monitored for unusual behavior. Software should remain current. Permissions should be evaluated periodically. Continuous maintenance ensures that security measures remain effective over time.

The tenth layer is adaptability. Technology evolves rapidly. New threats emerge regularly. Effective cybersecurity plans must remain flexible. Users should expect change and prepare to adapt accordingly. Adaptability allows security strategies to remain relevant despite evolving environments.

Risk management serves as the framework connecting all these layers. Every security decision involves balancing risks, costs, convenience, and benefits. Effective users do not attempt to eliminate every possible risk. Instead, they identify the most significant threats and allocate resources appropriately. This practical approach supports long-term success.

A cybersecurity master plan should also include personal goals. Different individuals prioritize different outcomes. Some focus primarily on privacy. Others prioritize financial security, business continuity, family protection, or professional reputation. Understanding personal priorities helps guide decision-making and resource allocation.

Automation can strengthen cybersecurity when used thoughtfully. Automatic updates, backup systems, account alerts, security monitoring tools, and password managers reduce dependence on memory and improve consistency. Automation helps ensure that important tasks occur regularly.

However, automation should complement rather than replace awareness. Technology provides valuable support, but informed judgment remains essential. Users should understand the systems they rely upon and maintain oversight of critical security functions.

One powerful aspect of a master plan is simplicity. Complex systems often fail because they become difficult to maintain. Effective security strategies balance thoroughness with practicality. Simple habits consistently followed usually outperform elaborate systems that are neglected over time.

Long-term success depends upon sustainability. Security practices should fit naturally within daily routines. Habits that require excessive effort are difficult to maintain. The most effective cybersecurity plans become integrated into normal life rather than existing as separate activities.

Another important principle is continuous improvement. Security should evolve gradually through learning, evaluation, and refinement. Small improvements implemented consistently produce significant results over time. Cybersecurity mastery is achieved through progression rather than perfection.

The ultimate objective of a cybersecurity master plan is confidence. Individuals who understand their risks, implement appropriate protections, maintain awareness, and prepare for incidents experience less anxiety and greater control. They can focus on enjoying the benefits of technology without being consumed by fear of potential threats.

Technology will continue transforming society in remarkable ways. Mobile devices will become even more powerful. Artificial intelligence will influence daily life. Connected systems will expand. Opportunities will increase alongside risks. Individuals who integrate cybersecurity into a comprehensive, sustainable framework will be well-positioned to thrive in this environment.

Cybersecurity mastery is not defined by technical expertise alone. It is defined by preparation, consistency, resilience, and the ability to adapt. By integrating everything learned throughout this series into a unified defense system, users can build a secure digital foundation capable of supporting personal, professional, and financial success for years to come.

James always believed he was reasonably careful with technology

He updated his phone occasionally, used passwords for important accounts, and avoided obviously suspicious websites. Like many people, he considered himself safer than average. Yet he had never developed a comprehensive approach to cybersecurity.

Over the years, James encountered various digital challenges. A social media account was compromised. A credit card required replacement after fraudulent transactions appeared. A phishing email nearly fooled him. A family member downloaded a suspicious application that caused security concerns.

Each incident was handled individually.

Each problem was solved separately.

Yet James never stepped back to examine the bigger picture.

One afternoon, while attending a professional development seminar, he listened to a cybersecurity expert discuss the concept of integrated defense systems. The speaker explained that successful cybersecurity depends on creating multiple layers of protection that work together rather than relying on isolated solutions.

The idea resonated immediately.

James realized his approach lacked structure. He had security measures in place, but they existed independently. There was no master plan connecting them.

Inspired by the presentation, he decided to conduct a comprehensive review of his digital life.

The process began with a simple inventory. He listed devices, accounts, applications, financial services, cloud storage platforms, communication tools, and connected systems. The results surprised him. Over the years, he had accumulated dozens of accounts and services he rarely used.

Some accounts had weak passwords.

Others lacked multi-factor authentication.

Several applications had unnecessary permissions.

A few devices were overdue for updates.

Individually, none of these issues seemed severe. Collectively, however, they created substantial risk.

James began building his cybersecurity master plan.

First, he strengthened authentication. Every important account received a unique password stored within a password manager. Multi-factor authentication was enabled wherever possible.

Next, he reviewed applications and permissions. Unused software was removed. Permissions were restricted. Privacy settings were updated.

Then he focused on backups and recovery planning. Important files were backed up automatically. Recovery procedures were documented. Emergency contacts and account information were organized securely.

The process took several weeks.

More importantly, it changed how James thought about cybersecurity.

Rather than reacting to problems as they appeared, he began managing risk proactively.

Months later, a major data breach affected one of the online services he used. News reports warned that customer information had been exposed.

Several years earlier, the announcement would have caused significant anxiety.

This time, James remained calm.

The compromised account used a unique password.

Multi-factor authentication was enabled.

Monitoring alerts were active.

Backup procedures existed.

The incident required attention, but it did not become a crisis.

The experience reinforced the value of preparation.

As his confidence grew, James expanded his efforts to include family members. Together, they reviewed devices, discussed scams, improved authentication practices, and created household security procedures.

One evening, his teenage daughter received a message appearing to originate from a popular social media platform. The message claimed her account would be suspended unless she verified credentials immediately.

Because of previous family discussions, she recognized several warning signs and ignored the message.

James realized that cybersecurity education creates benefits extending far beyond individual users.

Knowledge becomes protection.

Habits become defense.

Awareness becomes resilience.

Several years later, James faced another challenge when his smartphone was stolen during a business trip.

Although losing the device was frustrating, the incident unfolded far differently than it might have in the past.

The device was protected by strong authentication.

Remote management tools were enabled.

Sensitive information was encrypted.

Backup systems preserved important data.

Within hours, security procedures were activated. Within days, operations returned to normal.

The experience demonstrated how multiple layers of protection work together.

No single security measure solved the problem.

Instead, the combined effect of numerous preparations minimized the impact.

As technology continued evolving, James periodically reviewed and updated his master plan. New devices were incorporated. New services were evaluated. Emerging threats were considered.

The plan evolved, but its core principles remained stable.

Awareness.

Preparation.

Authentication.

Privacy.

Resilience.

Adaptability.

Continuous improvement.

Looking back, James realized the greatest benefit was not technical.

It was psychological.

He no longer felt overwhelmed by cybersecurity.

He no longer reacted to every news headline with concern.

He understood the risks, implemented reasonable protections, and maintained confidence in his ability to respond effectively.

Technology continued creating new opportunities for business, communication, education, and personal growth. Because he had established a strong cybersecurity foundation, he could embrace those opportunities with greater freedom.

His master plan did not eliminate every risk.

Nothing could.

What it provided was something far more valuable.

Control.

Control over his information.

Control over his decisions.

Control over his response to challenges.

Control over his digital future.

And in an increasingly connected world, that control became one of the most important assets he possessed.

Final Thoughts: Your Journey to Advanced Mobile Cybersecurity Mastery

As we reach the conclusion of *Advanced Mobile Cybersecurity and Digital Defense*, it is important to reflect on the incredible transformation that can occur when knowledge is combined with awareness, preparation, and action. Cybersecurity is often portrayed as a highly technical discipline reserved for specialists, government agencies, or large corporations. However, one of the most important lessons throughout this book is that cybersecurity is fundamentally about people. Technology may create risks, but human decisions determine how those risks are managed. Every user has the ability to improve their security posture, strengthen their defenses, and take greater control of their digital life.

The modern smartphone is one of the most powerful tools ever created. It provides instant communication, global access to information, financial management capabilities, healthcare resources, educational opportunities, navigation systems, entertainment platforms, and business tools. Yet the same device that creates tremendous convenience also contains enormous amounts of sensitive information. It serves as a gateway to personal identities, financial accounts, private conversations, and digital assets. Protecting that gateway has become one of the most important responsibilities of modern life.

Throughout this book, we explored the foundations of advanced mobile cybersecurity. We examined how mobile tracking systems operate and how personal information is collected through applications, networks, advertising systems, and connected devices. We learned that privacy is not simply about hiding information but about maintaining control over how information is gathered, stored, and shared. Understanding these processes empowers users to make informed decisions rather than unknowingly surrendering valuable personal data.

We also explored the critical role of authentication and identity protection. In today's digital economy, identities have become valuable targets for cybercriminals. Strong passwords, password managers, multi-factor authentication, account monitoring, and recovery planning provide powerful defenses against identity theft and account compromise. These tools may appear simple, but their impact can be profound. A single security habit can prevent months or even years of financial and emotional hardship.

Another key lesson involved malware, spyware, and malicious applications. Cybercriminals continuously develop new methods for infiltrating devices and collecting information. Fortunately, awareness, software updates, application reviews, secure browsing habits, and layered security controls significantly reduce exposure. Security is rarely about eliminating every possible threat. Instead, it is about creating barriers that make attacks more difficult and less likely to succeed.

The importance of resilience emerged repeatedly throughout this book. No security system is perfect. Devices can be lost, accounts can be targeted, and vulnerabilities can be discovered. Resilient individuals understand this reality and prepare accordingly. They maintain backups, create recovery plans, monitor accounts, and remain adaptable. Resilience transforms setbacks into manageable challenges rather than overwhelming crises.

One of the most valuable concepts discussed was the idea of a cybersecurity mindset. Technology changes rapidly, but principles remain remarkably stable. Awareness, verification, caution, responsibility, and continuous learning form the foundation of effective cybersecurity regardless of how devices or platforms evolve. Individuals who cultivate these habits position themselves for long-term success because they can adapt to new circumstances without abandoning core security principles.

The future will undoubtedly introduce new challenges. Artificial intelligence, smart homes, wearable devices, autonomous systems, digital currencies, and emerging communication technologies will create opportunities alongside risks. Some threats will become more sophisticated. Deepfakes may become increasingly convincing. Social engineering attacks may become more personalized. Privacy concerns may continue expanding as data collection grows. Yet individuals who understand cybersecurity fundamentals will remain prepared to respond effectively.

One encouraging reality is that cybersecurity knowledge compounds over time. Every lesson learned improves future decision-making. Every security habit strengthens overall resilience. Every successful defense reinforces confidence. Unlike many areas of life where effort produces temporary results, cybersecurity education often delivers lasting benefits that continue generating value for years.

Another important takeaway is that cybersecurity extends beyond individual protection. Family members, friends, coworkers, clients, and communities all benefit when individuals practice responsible security behaviors. Knowledge shared with others can prevent scams, reduce losses, and improve collective resilience. Cybersecurity becomes more powerful when it spreads through conversations, mentorship, and education.

Many people approach cybersecurity with fear. They worry about hackers, surveillance, identity theft, and emerging threats. While caution is appropriate, fear should never become the defining characteristic of digital life. The purpose of cybersecurity is not to create anxiety. It is to create confidence. Confidence comes from understanding risks, implementing protections, and preparing for challenges. The more informed and prepared individuals become, the less intimidating the digital world appears.

Confidence also creates freedom. Secure individuals can embrace technology more comfortably because they understand how to use it responsibly. They can explore opportunities, conduct business, communicate globally, and manage finances online without constantly worrying about every potential threat. Security and freedom are not opposing forces. Effective security enables greater freedom by reducing uncertainty.

Throughout history, every major technological advancement has introduced new responsibilities. The digital age is no different. Smartphones and connected devices have transformed society in extraordinary ways. They have created opportunities for learning, innovation, entrepreneurship, and global collaboration. Yet they also require users to become active participants in their own protection.

One of the most empowering lessons from this book is that effective cybersecurity does not require advanced technical expertise. It does not require expensive equipment or specialized training. It begins with awareness. It grows through education. It succeeds through consistent action. Small habits performed regularly often provide more protection than complex technologies used inconsistently.

As you move forward, consider conducting regular security reviews. Evaluate passwords. Review account settings. Audit application permissions. Update software. Verify backup systems. Monitor financial activity. Continue learning about emerging technologies and threats. These simple activities help maintain a strong security posture over time.

Remember that cybersecurity is a journey rather than a destination. There will always be new technologies to learn, new threats to understand, and new opportunities to explore. Continuous improvement is more important than perfection. Progress, not perfection, defines long-term success.

Most importantly, recognize that you possess significant influence over your digital future. Attackers may exist, vulnerabilities may appear, and risks may evolve, but informed users have powerful tools at their disposal. Knowledge, preparation, awareness, resilience, and adaptability remain among the strongest defenses available.

The Mobile Security & App Protection Academy series was designed to provide practical guidance for navigating an increasingly connected world. By applying the principles discussed throughout these books, you can strengthen your defenses, protect your privacy, secure your digital identity, and build confidence in your ability to manage technology safely.

As technology continues transforming society, your greatest asset will not be any specific device, application, or security tool. Your greatest asset will be your ability to think critically, learn continuously, adapt effectively, and take responsibility for your digital life.

Cybersecurity is ultimately about empowerment.

It is about protecting opportunities.

It is about preserving privacy.

It is about strengthening resilience.

It is about creating freedom through preparation.

And most importantly, it is about ensuring that technology remains a tool that serves you rather than a risk that controls you.

Thank you for investing in your cybersecurity education. May the knowledge you have gained throughout this journey help you navigate the digital world with confidence, awareness, resilience, and success for many years to come.

www.ingramcontent.com/pod-product-compliance
Lightning Source LLC
LaVergne TN
LVHW030727061126
851857LV00019B/2025
* 9 7 9 8 2 4 0 8 1 5 1 4 0 *